Mother's Faith

{Second Edition}

Books by Mrs. White

Mother's Faith

For The Love of Christian Homemaking

Cover photo - A parlour window from Mrs. White's
Vermont home.

Mother's Faith

*Essays, Lamentations and Encouragement
From a Christian Mother of Waywards*

By Mrs. Sharon White

The Legacy of Home Press
puritanlight@gmail.com

Mother's Faith

The content of this book is gathered from previously published posts from "The Legacy of Home" blog, written by Mrs. Sharon White. These were published during the years of 2009 to 2012.

The Legacy of Home Press
ISBN-13: 978-0615792217
ISBN-10: 0615792219
Mother's Faith {Second Edition}

Hidden Tears in a Teenager's Eyes

I've seen it so many times. It comes out as anger. It is demanding. It is harsh. It is irritating. But the truth is all hidden.

Many teens, when having a bad day or going through a difficult time, become abrasive. They even do this to the people they love.

But underneath are hidden tears.

May God give us the patience and compassion to bear the burden of their pain.

Introduction

Christian Mothers today are often struggling with having a happy home because of wayward teenagers. These mothers have spent years praying, teaching, and training their children in godliness. They have a great hope for a godly family and for children who grow up to bring joy to their hearts.

Instead, many teenagers and young adults have periods of waywardness. Their pain, their trials, and their choices bring weeping and sorrow to their godly mothers. But this is not the best way to face the trials of mothering older ones.

"*Mother's Faith*" is designed to help comfort these mothers. It is designed to inspire courage and bring them joy.

This book contains a collection of essays, which were specifically written by this mother of five, in the midst of my own sorrow and trials, over the course of 3 years.

This is a plain, small paperback book, but packed with an important, ongoing message: *Mother's Faith* must never waver, no matter what the waywards do in the home. Mother will one day reap a harvest of joy.

This book will help give you a holy patience.

Blessings
Mrs. White

March 25, 2013, Vermont

Table of Contents:

When Mother's Heart is Breaking

Remember when the children were little? They were so sweet and kind. They loved reading the Bible with Mother and singing hymns. Going to church with them was wonderful. At night, the family said their prayers and the children were tucked into bed for the night. Mother would stand in the doorway and watch them sleep, with a contented sigh. . . *Life was easier then.*

When children get older, Mother's heart is constantly breaking. She may find herself weeping more and more. It is hard to watch children grow up to want what this world offers. It is hard to see them *walk away* from their Bibles, and not want to read with Mother anymore.

There are going to be phases. There will be good and bad times. During the roughest moments, Mother may almost feel paralyzed by sorrow. It is hard to have courage in such times. It is hard to keep smiling, or be calm and patient. It is then that we must read more and more about long-suffering and mercy. There will be days when Mother will pray for each of her children, that it will hurt so much, *because of the sorrow*, she may want to stop. Yet, she cannot give up.

Perhaps during the early morning devotions, before the sun is up, Mother will spend more time praying for each child, begging God to keep them on the Heavenly Path. . . Not all will stray. Yet some may glance at the world and wonder....

Mother can pray for their protection. Then she must remember that the burden is too heavy for her to bear alone. She must leave it to God.

The Note in Mother's Pocket

Throughout the day, worries often come to mother's mind. She may be troubled about *this* child, or *that* one. She may be concerned about finances or stormy weather. She may be worried about her husband, or how to handle some difficulty.

These thoughts can make her shaky, sad, and fearful. But the wise mother has learned a little secret. *She keeps a note in her pocket.*

This note is a little reminder of the answers to all her troubles. She will go about her homemaking duties, washing clothes, polishing furniture, doing dishes, tending the children and making food. Every so often, she will reach in her pocket and remember the note. *This soothes her rising fears.*

Sometimes, when times get really tough, mother will take the note out of her pocket. She will lay it down on the table before her, and she will read it. Seeing the words on the note comfort her greatly. Then she will put the paper back in that *special place,* where she can carry it around everywhere.

There is something from Scripture in I Samuel 17:47. It is a very precious message. No matter what our troubles; no matter what Goliaths we face; or trials our children have to face, ". . . *the battle is the Lord's. . .*"

. . . And these are the very words on Mother's note.

Mother's Silent Influence in the Home

There seems to be two kinds of Christians.

1. Regular Christians and
2. Spiritual Christians.

I'm going to explain my theory here and also how it relates to Mama and her quiet influence.

Regular Christians

These dear people go to church regularly, have morals, and do their best to live the Christian life. They are God's children and He loves them dearly. But there is something lacking. This has nothing to do with their path to heaven but with their life here on earth. They have never fully experienced the sorrow, the wisdom and the blessed joy of weeping in God's spiritual arms. This comes in time. This comes over a period of many years.

Spiritual Christians

These are the "white haired" saints of old (even if they are not yet elderly). These people have been through the fiery trials of life and have clung to the Lord through it all. They have a Spiritual heart; a hunger for the Master and for Heaven. They yearn for it. They weep for, seemingly, no reason. You can hear them singing quietly to themselves while they go about their work. When you look at them, you almost see the angels surrounding them with comfort and heavenly love. There is something about them that reminds one of Moses, as he came off the Mount after meeting with God to receive the Ten Commandments. The faces of these Spiritual Christians shine (Exodus 34:29), as if they have just been in the company of the Precious Lord Himself. This is the earthly state that all Christians aspire to.

When our children are growing up in our homes, we want them to see Mama living for her God. They do not know Him literally yet, but they will be drawn to Him by watching a Godly Mother.

The other day, I was in my living room cutting out an apron pattern and doing some sewing. I listened to Bill Monroe on the radio, singing the old song *"I am a Pilgrim."* And my heart soared with joy. My 19 year old daughter got all dressed up to go out for the evening. She was full of the cares of this life and she was happy. I smiled at her. We old people do that to the young. We smile at their happiness. But then she did this little dance and I gasped and had this sharp, brutal pain in the center of my chest and said so. She ran over to me laughing, "Oh, Mom, you are so cute. I will never do that dance again." -*How precious-*

My children tell me that there are things they will not share with Grandpa (my Dad). He is a godly man from the old south and he loves His Bible and Spiritual things. He would be deeply offended and spiritually wounded (saddened) by some of their worldly cares (*exploits*?). But when they say they will tell me things, or let me read their tell-all books, or listen to their worldly songs, I get this sad feeling. That I compromise with them perhaps? That I am not as strong as my Dad? Would I rather they shared all these things with me or that they held some back out of respect for a saintly mother? I prefer to be considered more like their Grandpa, and strive for this more and more every day.

Our children are puzzled by the faith. They know God, they believe in Him but they do not have that Spiritual connection yet. They are but babes. All goodness and holy striving will come for them in time. Yet, they can watch Mama as she goes about her day, loving her Bible, loving sermons, godly fellowship and godly music. They will notice her *aversion*, more and more to the world, until she reaches that state of an "almost" perfection of the soul; where she is being prepared for heaven. All the worldly cares mean nothing anymore. This is the strongest testimony to our young. They observe all this and they want it, but don't know how to get it. They will ponder these things in their hearts and when the time comes, they will cling to the silent witness of Mama's life and be led to her Glorious God.

A Mother of Sinners

It is a somber and sad day when Mother realizes her children are sinners. There is something called "The Depravity of Man" - and a "sin nature." These are things our children will fight against, each day, for the rest of their lives. It causes them great pain and suffering. . . *But it hurts Mom the most.*

The sad realization is when you have young adults and teenagers who try so hard to walk the road of righteousness, but keep getting distracted by the world. They come home full of adventurous experiences- some thrilling, some heartbreaking - but there is sadness in their eyes, and *marks* from the thorns. There is no *pure holiness* in them, like you once thought there would be, when they were *baby-cherubs* in your eyes. There is dirt and filth because. . frankly . . . your children have been *dangerously* playing in the world. And it will tear your heart out. . .

Others will see and mock. They are like closet-Pharisees who think they are above depravity. This is the saddest thing of all - when your fellow Christian man gives up on your family and walks away- as if *you*, as the mother, did something wrong.

But I know a secret. . .

It is to *never give up*. I learned this in profound ways from some very precious Mothers - Emma, Erma and Edith:

Emma (1950's)

Emma was Old Order Amish and became a widow at a young age. She was left with six children to raise, alone at home, and with the help of her Amish community. She watched as young people experimented with the rules and "English" world around them. She was terrified as they did things that were dangerous to their souls. She prayed in secret and received constant comfort and reassurance from The Master. But most of her children left the church to join more progressive churches. The culture was rapidly changing and it was seeping into the Amish world. One of the important things I learned from Emma was this:

She did not try to convince her children of the old ways - *she lived it.* When her teenagers and young adults were living questionable lives, she let it all play out and let them learn their lessons. Why did she do this? She knew the Holy Spirit was working in their lives and God was in control. While she certainly advised them and got help and support from the elders, her daily practice as a mother was to let them learn to make decisions for themselves so they could grow. The hardest lesson I learned from Emma was that, since we live in a rapidly decaying culture, our children are not always going to follow our old paths. They are facing new challenges in each generation - new temptations - and living in a culture that we never would have imagined. Through it all, and despite the pain, she knew how to remain Amish. The lesson: stand fast in your faith, mother, regardless of the path your children take.

Erma (1960's)

In Erma's time, there was free love. Teenagers were spitting on the ground their parents walked on, and forsaking traditional family. They were shacking up and doing all manner of drugs. They hated

our country and hated decency. They
brought a downfall of horror to our society.
When they did this, they only said, "peace,"
but they were deluded.

Erma had an amazing sense of humor, as
a mother. She was a beloved columnist who
shared her life with millions of readers. She
encouraged them and made them laugh,
even when they wanted to cry. Through all
the pain and frustration of raising her
children to be decent, God fearing citizens,
she did the most important thing of all - she
did not give up.

Edith (1970's)

As the war on our culture raged, feminism
(or as some call it, - Nazi-feminism) was
raging strong. Edith, the traditional
housewife, who was dedicated to her family,
putting them first above all things- had a
feminist daughter and a liberal son-in-law.
The amazing thing about Edith is that she
stayed who she was. She did not bend to

the will of society -she did not become like her daughter - she remained a steadfast example of home, family and motherhood - and she did it all without pushing her views on anyone. She did it in silence. Her example meant more to a nation, on that television screen, even though the show was meant to belittle her. Even Erma loved her and said *the world needed more Ediths.*

No matter what we see in our children, on the surface, we have no idea what kind of work God is doing behind the scenes. He is laying the groundwork for their future. He is allowing them to wallow in things in order to gain experience in life, and to know and understand heartache. He is teaching them things we could never teach them. So, *dear Mother of sinners*, no matter what is going on in the lives of your children, remember this - a virtuous godly mother who is *unflinching* in her faith, while full of flaws herself, is the greatest testimony to her children than any words you could utter.

Mother, *ignore the Pharisees*, and stay strong and brave. In the very end, your children will rise up and call you blessed.

"Blessed is the man that trusteth in the Lord, and whose hope the Lord is." Jeremiah 17:7

The Sum of Godly Motherhood

Someone asked Mother Teresa if she ever got discouraged working with the poor in Calcutta. They wondered if seeing no success in her daily tasks ever made her feel like she wasn't doing worthwhile work. Her answer was that she was not called to a mission of success, but *a mission of mercy* - a mission of work.

I see this as what we mothers are doing in the home. We are labouring in difficult fields, training and caring for our children. Sometimes we encounter stubbornness, wilfulness and foolish decisions, as our children learn and grow into adulthood. They don't see all the work we do behind the scenes - we struggle with drought, too much rain, wildlife, and a multitude of weeds who come in and try to destroy our crops. We toil in these fields on a daily basis and often we don't see success. We wait. . . and we pray. . . and we beg God to give us patience and mercy so that we can continue on each day. But we rarely see our results until many years later.

The Bible says that children rise up and call their virtuous Mother blessed. Often, those same children do not realize the sacrifice and toil and prayers that went into all her work. They also don't realize all she did, through all those years, as she submitted to God in her work, with all trust and faith; that these very acts, helped create the virtuous character she possesses in her old age.

Trouble With Teenagers

In this modern culture, teenagers are not who they used to be. *Remember the 1950's when children were respectful and family-oriented?* Those were idyllic days; Fast forward to 2010. We have a rebellious, angry generation who are drawn to ungodliness and the world around them.

Why am I sitting here at my computer, in the middle of the night, writing about this? Because I am suffering. Normally, in this house, we have peace and joy. But *right now*, all is not well. I have chest pains, anxiety attacks and just cannot cope. I need peace. I need to write through my pain so I can get through the night.

I have spent all my years as a mother sowing seeds of righteousness and godliness into my children. *But the harvest is wounded.* Some of my older children are going through mighty trials and I can't handle the ride. I am weary. I lost my sense of humor. I am speechless. I am mute.

But I am going to turn this around. I am going to give you some ideas of things I've done in the past to get through the rough storms. I will do this to regain my bearings. It is my hope that this writing will clear my aching soul and make me well again:

Photo Album.

Whenever one of my teenage daughters was giving me a hard time, I would look through old pictures of her, from when she was a precious little girl. I would smile at the image of her sweet, innocent face. What a treasure! I would remember all her fun antics and my tears would be gone. I would remember that there is a child inside that hardened heart and the difficult moment would pass - then all would be well again.

I plan to make photo albums for the rest of the children, so I have more of an eternal perspective, rather than a struggle with "right now." I want to remember that they *will* grow out of the difficult phase and things *will* get better. The pictures help keep me calm, and soften my heart for them.

She is the Cheese.

Have you seen that commercial on television about the cheese? There is this large, round block of cheese. A technician, wearing a white coat, walks into the room. He is holding a clipboard with a checklist that says:

_____ Ready.

_____ Not Ready.

As soon as he walks in, the cheese starts making fun of him and laughing. The Technician takes his pen and marks off "not ready." When he turns to walk away, we see a "kick-me" sign on his back. We are told that the cheese is not yet mature.

The Tech walks in on another day and the cheese is still being foolish. The Tech walks away again. Then finally, on the last day, he walks in and the cheese says something like, "How are you today sir?" The cheese is polite. The Tech marks "Ready" and says the cheese has aged and is now mature.

The other day, one of my children was hostile, and acting up. I scolded that child and remained calm. I let the moment pass. Then I told the child that she was "the cheese" and I laughed and smiled and explained the commercial. It was my way of coping through the moment and we all enjoyed the comparison. Everything was okay.

A Sense of Humor Rather than giving in to Anger.

I can't always be happy.... (big surprise, right?) . . But, I do try to keep my sense of humor. One day last week, I had a frustrated teen yell, and then storm out the back door. I didn't know where this teen was going, so I went out after this child. I found him just standing outside in the back yard.

"*What are you doing*?" I asked. He just looked at me, held up his hands and said, in an aggravated tone, "*I'm right here!*"

I smiled and said, "*Well, I didn't know where you were going, or what you were going to do. What did you expect me to think with that grand exit of yours?"*

Suddenly, we both laughed. Everything was okay. The bad mood was gone and we were smiling.

Sad Stories.

I was sitting in the car, reading a precious story. It was about this godly Jewish mother who had three sons. She raised them to be pious. Throughout their childhood, they attended Shul every single day. They also attended Jewish schools and were taught to live out their faith. But those boys grew up and married secular wives. They had secular children. They stopped practicing the faith they had known and cherished. They had been pulled away by worldly wives. This broke their mother's heart. One day, when this Mother died, the grown men were devastated. They went over the eulogy and funeral plans with the Rabbi and begged him to explain what a wonderful, godly woman their mother was. They were so heartbroken and wanted their mother to be praised. Later, as they stood at the funeral, they could not be consoled. They wept, and each one touched the casket as it was being lowered into the ground. One of the men whispered, through heavy tears, "We're sorry Mama."

My heart broke and I wept in the car as I read that. You see, it isn't about me... I must learn the lesson- the lesson that none of this is personal. The trials my children are going through is God working in and through their lives to mold them and make them into his image. And yet, the fiery furnace *singes* me at times and I am hurt. But I must remain peaceful and trust my precious Lord that all will be well in the end.

I must retain my composure and stop letting their foolishness get to me. I must take it to God, let go of it, and then laugh and be cheerful and enjoy my Bible, prayers and hymns. One day, these children will be mature. They will also be *spiritually* mature and I will finally reap that harvest I have been waiting for all these years.

Mother's Hope

I created a little book of hope. . . I had to survive. . . Trials at home, with my teenagers and adult children were wearing me out. I was often crying, sad, and unable to cope. Their pain became my pain. Their struggles with the world overwhelmed me. Their frustrations and anger with growing up, came out as attacks within the family. It wasn't okay and I was not handling it well.

This book of hope is like the old time mother's vintage homekeeping book. This is the kind of thing that is handwritten full of advice, recipes, and newspaper clippings.

But it is not about cooking. It is about motherhood.

I have a pretty purple binder. I am decorating the cover with Bible verses, drawings, pictures of peaceful scenes and the simple words - *Mother's Hope.* Inside there are 6 dividers tabs. I have five children, ages 13 - 23. Each child will have a section in the back. I will tape pictures of them when they were precious, smiling babies to help me remember what is inside that grown soul standing before me, fighting with the world. I will remember that I am to mother the child inside them. I will write prayers for them. I will put their letters to me and their cute sayings in that section, as they happen. I will keep filling it up each day or each week or each month or however often I need *hope.* The front section will be full of beautiful thoughts, Biblical promises, prayers, quotes, clippings and ideas to inspire me. And there will be a journal. Yes, a journal. . to remind me of the victories and the miracles. This will build my shaky faith.

Why do I need this? I remember staying up all night with a sick baby. We would stand near the steam of the shower just so the baby could breathe. I would stay awake all night like that and then pace the front porch so the infant could breathe-in the fresh night air. I remember being so tired, so weak, and in desperate need of a break. But I would pray and beg God for strength. *I never once thought of myself or what I needed.* I just took care of that baby with all the love and courage I could muster.

I remember another night, with a different baby. This one was throwing up and only 9 months old. This baby needed to sleep sitting up. So I set up the car seat and settled that baby down next to me. I planned to stay awake all night to make sure he was okay. But he kept throwing up. So I picked him up and paced the living room floor; Back and forth, back and forth. He stopped throwing up and fell into a deep sleep. Whenever I tried to lay him back down, he would wake up. So I paced, holding that baby all night long. I remember seeing the moon out the back window. I remember how dark and silent the world was at that time. I remember praying and begging God for mercy and courage and for strength. I remember my legs shaking. But I kept going. *I never thought of myself,* but to ask for endurance. It was selfless. It was a Mother's duty.

Now that my children are older - teens and adults, I realize I have lost my way. I have become selfish without even realizing it. I am not dealing with sickness this time, but attitudes. I am dealing with their struggles, sin natures and frustrations. When these bad moments come, I go off to rest. I say I need a break. I tell them to talk to Dad about it. I escape. I go into survival mode. But I <u>never once</u> ask God to give me *strength* and *courage* and *endurance*. My immediate thoughts are survival for ME. It is selfish. I must remember that God will provide the rest, when I do the work.

This is why I need hope. . . This is why I need my book. . . It will be my reflective reminder of my job as a Mother. It is a tool to help me *remember* the ministry of motherhood.

Who Will Weep For You Now?

I read this story once, where a travelling preacher stopped by the side of the road to see a Father and his older children, weeping and distraught. They explained that the wife had died leaving the children motherless. The husband described his wife as a *precious saint*, who had prayed for them all. . . and loved them all dearly. The husband cried out to the preacher, feeling so alone and abandoned, saying, "*Who will pray for us now?*"

The preacher led them to the Lord and encouraged them on their way. This greatly comforted them.

Over the years, as I have visited with people on my way to church, I have heard them call out to me, "*Please say a prayer for me, while you are there.*" This gives them a good, safe feeling, knowing that someone is on their side, before the Lord. . . Knowing that someone is there pleading for their well-being. And this is good.

Mothers are known for weeping in prayer for their children and for their families. Mother's *love* and *concern* is so great . . . and so strong . . . that those kinds of tearful, heart-breaking, prayers bring about great things from God.

Grown children know that each day, at *the appointed time of family worship*, their Mother is back at home, praying for them. They know Mother is weeping when they do wrong. They know that Mother would be heartbroken if sin got a hold of them, or if danger was in their path. These children feel as if a guardian angel is watching over them, when they have their saintly mother's prayers to hold them up.

But what happens when Mother is gone? What happens when that Mother has passed-on to her eternal rest? Who will pray for them now?

Will you, like the family on the side of the road, be led to the Lord and carry on the beauty of the Mother's prayers? May it be so.

And you, *who are the precious Mothers,* will you keep your eyes on Heaven and your hearts on things not of this world, that your prayers be not hindered? May God help us all!

The Mother Who Will Not Accept Reality

Our children walk in a dangerous world. They get into all kinds of mischief, often *soberly* and *intentionally.* Some think, "Well, this is who they are." Or, "It is their choice in life." That is the common reality.

But the mother who has holy ideals for her offspring, the mother who seeks and strives to see them walking a well-lit heavenly path, will not accept any of the bad.

This kind of mother does not pray *dry prayers.* She does not pray by rote or through cold, generalizations. Her prayers are heartfelt and comfortingly urgent. They are specific and precious. *Yet they come not from her own mind.*

A Mother, in a lukewarm state, cannot utter solemn prayers. She is incapable because she is full of "self" in her normal state of human nature. But the mother who takes one little step towards a holy life, such as spending a morning in Bible reading, poring over the hymn book, or raptly listening to a godly sermon, has the most humble, heartbreaking prayers coming from her soul.

These kinds of prayers touch the Master.

Can you just image what would happen if we truly understood verses like this:

"For the righteous Lord loveth righteousness; his countenance doth behold the upright."
(Psalm 11:7)

Imagine the feeble efforts of the mother saints, with humble hearts seeking God. Imagine Heaven's light of glory, and joy, shining on them and bringing them the beauty and awe just like Moses when he came off from the Mount after spending time with God. He needed a veil because the glory of the Lord, which he had been sitting by and warming his soul, had been so strong that it brought fear and trembling to onlookers.

Imagine if we never settled for the reality we see before us. Imagine if we refused to accept sin and wrong paths in our children. Imagine if we went to our Heavenly Father, warmed ourselves in His holy presence and constantly begged Him for regeneration and sanctification in our own lives and in those of our children.

Oh, what a Godly Generation this would bring!

Living With Heathens

John Walton didn't go to church. I never understood why. His wife went. His children went. And even his parents (Grandpa and Grandma Walton) went every week with the family. Why didn't John go?

On a recent episode of *The Waltons*, a new preacher moved into town. John went to visit him and said, good naturedly, "I've been a heathen too long. Don't try to convert me." The preacher laughed. He knew John was teasing. Everyone in town knew John was a pillar of the community. He was a man of integrity, a man with strong values, and an inspiring father. He had tremendous wisdom and lived out God's commandments. He prayed with his family and encouraged them to go to church. But he wouldn't go himself.

Some wives have husbands like John. They have children like John. Or, perhaps they live with family members who act like literal heathens. Maybe they don't read the Bible, or openly pray. Maybe they won't go to church and seem unhappy in their souls. All these things can affect the godly mother in the home.

I've sensed the "seeming" burden of religious education fall on Olivia Walton. I've seen her scold the children for wrongdoing and I've heard her teach those children the Bible. She had Grandma Walton to back her up. And even Grandpa was a laid-back, but dedicated religious man. Was this burden difficult for Olivia? What was it like living in a home where all family members were not all out for God, in a visual, literal sense?

But this isn't the issue. . .

The problem is when Mother is so caught up in the sorrows of others, that she cannot focus on her own soul. She can easily spend much of her time worrying, pleading, begging and weeping for the "heathens" in her life, that she forgets to cultivate a relationship with the Lord.

The saying goes, "*More is caught than taught.*" Mother must keep her eyes on heaven and learn to trust and have faith that God is taking care of it all. She must spend her daily life seeking to be closer to Him, and not being distracted by earthly cares or worldly worries.

The fruit of this effort is a bright, warm light comforting those around her and guiding them Heavenward.

The light does the guiding, not her words.

It has been said that we are vessels for the Master's use. He works through us, not because of us. We must remember each and every day, and keep reminding ourselves, over and over again, that we need More Love, More Focus, More Dedication to The Almighty and that is our main purpose in life. We have to remember that no matter what the "seeming" heathens do, we have to live His way, even if it looks like no one else is.

Mother's Glory

One of the greatest delights of motherhood is taking pride in our young children. We work hard to bathe, feed, educate, train and clothe them. They are like precious cherubs who delight us and give us joy. We love and adore them.

Our most difficult task, however, is instilling virtue and moral values into their characters. We take them to Sunday school and Church events. We read the Bible and pray with them. We make Bible time and family worship a daily habit, hoping and praying it will take root in their souls and give them the peace that passeth all understanding, and lead them to their eternal home.

As time goes on, our little ones get into the middle years and things get harder. They begin taking different paths and making childish decisions that cause them harm. When they are teenagers and young adults, they may fall into a great many trials. *And this will make a mother weep.* She may go into a deep despair and be heartbroken for many years.

The bravest of mothers will smile through this dark time, and bring as much heavenly light into the home as she possibly can. She will still seek holiness and will endure, knowing the dawn will soon come.

One great day, Mother's glory will shine forth. The glory is - *finally realizing* that it is God that molds and shapes a holy soul, and it is HE who gets the glory. If the child had grown, with ease, under mothers dedicated care, without a fault or a trial, then her skills and talents would have received all the praise. Nay, *let it not be so.*

That family may have shined here on this earth, but the brighter reward is the holy warmth of the Lord which shapes the souls of mother's children. It is the mother's *tears* and *work* and *turmoil* through the years that is praised. But the final result, *the reality of Mother's glory*, is the humble and broken gratefulness of seeing God work in their lives, of God stepping in and doing the miracles, and of God making holy citizens out of the descendants in Mother's house.

The glory is the Lord's. Remember this the next time you fall into weeping for your children.

Don't Let It Become A House Of Sorrow

I was standing in my parlour, *just standing there*, in misery. So many wonderful things were happening and then this. It was another trial; One that brought tears of frustration and pain. Mr. White and my boys helped us through it. They were the protectors, and the problem solvers. But I was still *fearful* and shaky.

John walked over to me. He is 15. He opened his Bible and started to read Psalm 23. Matt (19) had a hand on the door to go outside. He paused and listened. Suddenly all was calm. None of it mattered anymore.

We were comforted and soothed. We could move on. We could forgive, offer grace and mercy, and let the Lord handle the trial.

Have you ever seen those medicine commercials for those suffering from depression? I often watch the people sitting in the chair, or not getting out of bed, and think, I would LOVE to do that! I would love to sit near a window all day, staring out at the landscape, and not have to worry, or do anything. And this is the *temptation*, when the whole world seems to be crashing down on us. However, these moments of suffering are passing. They don't last! They are the dark night. We have to fight our way through them, using our weak flashlight (our positive attitude) until we make it to the dawn.

Every single home has troubles that come and go. We will have calm times, and happy times, and joyful times. Sadly, these may only last a few moments, but we have to hang on to them. We remember them, and reminisce about them, and bring them back, to get us through those *other times.*

Last night, I opened my hymnbook and sang with John.   We sang, "*Bringing in the Sheaves.*"   We sang it over and over again. Singing these old hymns remind us that we will suffer in this life, but the reward will come. Our work will last. It is important. This is our comfort.

But please don't let the disappointments, financial worries, disagreements, or the sorrow for sins around us, bring down the gray hairs of sorrow on your homes. *Let them not be houses of mourning.* We have to do the work of smiling, laughing, joking and making light of things. We have to seek out the rainbows, and open the curtains to see the sunshine!

Each moment, each morning, let all bitterness and grudges fall away. Start new with a smile, and some love, and *a heart of cheerful service.* Make your home a happy place, despite the trouble. If you do that, you will be the greatest wife and mother on this earth!

The Last Witness of An Era

The culture around us is changing rapidly. Each generation becomes less and less recognizable to the last. There is a *craving* for the newest and the latest idea. Often Mothers are tempted to walk away from the old path and blend-in with the world around them.

We need mothers who will be a living example of the old ways. We need mothers with courage and discipline to stand strong in these times.

In my son's Karate class, the teacher will run to each student and try to knock him over. The student must always be on guard. He must stand tall and fixed. He must be unbending to resist the attack. This is the kind of strength we mothers need. The attack is the seduction of a worldly culture, which seeks materialism, partying, endless fun, and ungodly living. Mothers must be seeking to glorify God, rather than self. In this, we must walk the old paths and be the light to the world around us.

Have you ever met an older person who lived through World War II? Or have you met someone who lived through the great-depression? They are *the last of the witnesses* of those difficult times. They have seen many things. They have experienced many things. We learn from them. We watch how they live now, and hear them speak. . . and we get a glimpse into the reality of history. This is part of *seeking the old paths.*

This current era is changing rapidly. The music, the food, technology, family life, and social expectations are almost unrecognizable to previous generations. In order to keep godly culture alive, we must not conform to society around us. We must seek strength to be a witness of the era in which we now live. This is impossible to do alone. We need God's help.

"Resolution One: I will live for God. Resolution Two: If no one else does, I still will."
-Jonathan Edwards, 1703-1758

Like the Mothers Before Me

I stayed up late last night waiting for one of my children to come home. I sat in the quiet parlour near the fire and prayed. I prayed for *all* my children. It was a peaceful time. It had been a day of worry. These worries come from thinking about the "what ifs," which is caused from a lack of faith and trust in God.

Then I started thinking about the Mothers before me. These saints of old were strong in Christian courage. They were dedicated to living a godly life. This made me remember the example of Ruth Bell

Graham. She was an amazing inspiration to so many!

I want to share a couple of quotes from 2 of her 5 children:

"My mother was always bright and sparkly, even when she worried or would get only an hour or two of sleep at night. She might have been worrying about a student at college or a member of her Sunday school class - or me, like when I was growing up and wouldn't get home until 4:00 a.m. Mother never went to bed until all of us children were back in for the night. She has that bright, cheerful personality, and I believe it comes from her daily walk with the Lord." - Franklin Graham

"I believe that our heavenly Father, our Savior, saved my mother from loneliness because of her daily walk with the Lord Jesus. He was the love of her life. I saw that in her life. It was her love for the Lord Jesus; with whom she walks every day, that made me want to love Him and walk with Him like that." - Anne Graham Lotz

Mrs. Graham left quite a legacy. Her influence, writings, and life will continue to inspire many generations of mothers.

"Secret religion is the very soul of godliness." - C.H. Spurgeon

Seeking Godliness at Home

I have had some trials the last couple of days. But every night, I have been reading a few passages from "*Stepping Heavenward*" by Elizabeth Prentiss.

Lately, the main character's trials are mirroring my own. There can be turmoil in a home. It is hard for a Mother not to get emotional - either sad or angry, depending on what is happening around her.

But tonight, a glimpse of light has come to cheer me on. I will share a small part of the book. It is from the journal of "Katy":

"I see now why He has put some thorns into my domestic life; but for them I should be too happy to live. It does not seem just the moment to complain, and yet, as I can speak to no one, it is a relief to write about my trials."

I know this one little part doesn't make as much sense as reading the entire story. But what has come over me is the yearning for Heaven. We are always going to be dealing with petty things. There will always be the "town gossip," who speaks ill of the innocent. There will always be people who misunderstand or complain or frankly, those who are so careless; it does not concern them when they cause our suffering.

But my joy will always come from the Lord. If I can have that precious, cheerfulness in all things, I will be content. If I can just keep my moods in check, so that I can always be ever so happy (in my very soul), and not caught up in the world around me, my joy will always remain.

At that point, I can make my home a happy place, just because I am ever-cheerful. If only that were possible!! (smiles) Yet, it is my goal. I strive for it every single day. I search for it, I work for it, in daily religious duties - the only thing that keeps me sustained. But it is not enough. So I will keep doing more, throughout the day, to keep my heart focused - so that the things of earth will finally become dim.

How A Godly Mother May Guide an Imperfect Family

So many mothers have trials and sorrows.
They cry out to God because of wayward
children. Or, perhaps they shake their head
in despair when their young child continues
to do wrong. We need a country of strong,
encouraged mothers. We need Mothers to
understand that all children, *all people*,
have a sin nature. Our families will be
imperfect.

Whenever you see a lovely family of Bible
Hugging children- know you are only seeing
an image. Those children still sin and give
their parents trouble. Perhaps they bicker,
or disobey, or even lie. But they love their
Mother and they love their Bible. It doesn't

mean they are going to be perfect. Let's get that clear, first off.

Children silently observe all that Mother does. They know what she is really like. It cannot be hidden in the home. Mother, we need to know we cannot do any of this alone. We need our dear Lord and I will tell you how to find strength from Him.

1. Strive to live a simple, unworldly life. Find time for recreation for the sake of the body, but it must not be the consuming of one's life.

2. Read the Bible more than any other reading material. Read it to ponder. Read it while praying. Read it while weeping. Read it for strength.

3. Pray with all thy heart and soul and strength. Pray diligently throughout the day. Pray for each child by name. Pray for

courage. Pray for faith and love of God's holy way. Pray about everything.

4. Live out your commitments without wavering. Do what you promise to do, even if it causes you pain, exhaustion and suffering. You will be a shining example of a dedicated, responsible soul if you can be trusted to keep your word.

5. Work hard. Work with whatever you have been given to do. Work with all your strength and might- whether it be in your housekeeping, cooking, mothering, gardening or what have you. Do it with pride and commitment.

6. Talk about God with your children. Tell them about your prayers and the answers when they come. Show your children your total trust and faith in your Heavenly Father. Do this in normal, daily life- as things come up - rather than in forced conversations.

7. Offer Grace and Mercy to your children.
Do not hold grudges. Forgive at once!
Forgive even if they are still acting up!
Forgive, smile, show compassion and love
them with every bit of your strength.
Forgive them over and over and over again -
without end.

8. Speak life into your children. Lift them
up. Praise them and tell them how much
you love them and are grateful for them.

9. Do good things for your children. Make
an effort to cook their favorite meals and
make home a special place they want to be.
Make a pleasant and loving home for your
family. Do good things for them,
unconditionally - even if they are acting
troublesome. Show them love through your
actions.

10. Live out a godly life before them. Pray
openly. Read your Bible openly. Sing hymns
or listen to gospel music openly. Go to the

Master and fill your heart with love and holiness and then face your family, fully equipped to minister, while doing your homemaking tasks.

11. Confess your faults. If you are in a bad mood - tell them you are sorry. If you made a foolish decision- repent of it. Show them that none of us are flawless, but God has great mercy and we can only cling to him as the source of our hope.

12. Never bend. Know what your convictions are and do not change them with the times. Do not try to join in sinful, worldly living just to be friends with your children. You are the Mother. You are the example. You must stay strong and live out a godly, holy life before your family. Do not bend to their childish, immature worldly whims. I cannot stress this enough. Children will grow up, remembering your example. One day they will cling to the old ways and realize it was your source of

strength. Long after you are dead and gone, dear mother, they will remember your strong character and godly ways. Don't underestimate the power of a committed, godly life.

13. Realize that money and things are never going to be more important than one's convictions. If you are seeking money at the expense of your family, or at the expense of your moral values - pray and find a way to drop it as quickly as possible. Nothing is more important than the salvation of the souls of your children. Do not let money, things, or the world's standard of life destroy your only chance of bringing up godly children.

I want to paint an image of what this looks like in an old fashioned home. Mother has her daily duties. We thank God for her work, because it gives her something important to do. She cannot spend all day wasting time on television, constant eating and lounging. She needs to be about the Master's business - and that is the keeping of the home. She should pray for love for her job, so that it will shine through and bless those around her. I can see her right now, washing clothes, hanging them on the line. I see her humming and smiling while she makes supper. Now she is reading the Bible and sharing a verse or two that has blessed her. All her worries are cast on the Lord in prayer. She goes about her daily life, unhurried, and in peace. The children feel safe and secure because they know Mama is there.

Dear ones, our daily religious duties are an obligation. We do them whether or not we feel like it. It is what helps keep us on the straight and narrow. If we follow our own way, our own desires, we will be led astray. Perhaps we don't want to go to church. This is an enormous struggle in many homes. We don't want to go. But if we go out of obligation and gratefulness to God, we are setting an amazing example to our children.

We, as mothers, will have children of all ages, at all stages on their religious journey. Some have been saved, some are struggling in sin, some are confused, and some are under the chastening hand of God. We need to be there, praying, smiling, encouraging and seeing them through these rough years. We may be weeping now, as we work in the harvest fields, but in the end, we will rejoice, bringing our sheaves with us. All that matters, at the end of it all, is not the fun we had, or the worldly things we indulged in, or the money we earned. What matters is walking through the pearly gates, with the souls of our beloved children following us into heaven.

When Mother Feels Unappreciated

I am shaking this morning. I am weak and weary on this path of life. But I am in good spirits. I know where my source of comfort lies.

I worked very hard yesterday, while the family was all at home. I cleaned and baked and cooked and visited. It was taxing on my fragile body. I remember standing over the stove in the late afternoon and stirring the food in a pan. I was shaking then. I thought to myself, "*I am too old for this.*" I didn't feel young or energetic anymore. I did not have the endurance to do basic things. Then I thought of my own mother, *with a crown of silver* and a cane in her hand, and how she still cooks, even if she is shaking. (gentle smiles)

I asked my teenagers for help. They were occupied in the parlour, laughing and visiting and didn't understand my need for help. They had already done so much for me. It would have been easy for me to burst into tears (like a small, tired child) and collapse into a chair, but I prayed a little prayer and smiled, and said tenderly, "I just need a little help." One of them smiled and came to my assistance. I realize they see me, *a picture of health*, but don't have any idea of the deafness, the blindness, the aches, the shaking that goes on in this old mother. When they grumble and complain about helping (like all normal children), *they know not what they do*. They think mother is a tireless saint who can work miracles in the home and kitchen.

I once read about the troubles of Elizabeth Prentiss (1800's), in one of her books. She wrote about her struggle with frail health and how her children would gather around her for stories, or help, but they would elbow her and nudge her and cause her pain - *unknowingly.* It "cost her" dearly to be a mother, but was *worth every bit of pain.*

Patricia St. John, in her autobiography, spoke highly of her mother. She talked about how she and her siblings would giggle and laugh and make fun, at times, when her mother tried to teach them the Bible. Looking back she realized they had caused her heartache. That mother was greatly admired for her patience and loving guidance, *despite the trouble.*

There are many moments when I feel unappreciated. My greatest weapon to fight this dark thought is to smile and to pray and to keep going. . . I have already seen the fruits of my efforts, in my grown children, who are tender and loving and helpful. When they grow up, they no longer think as children. They are no longer focused on self, or unaware of the pain of others. This is why I love the Biblical prayer, "*Remember not the sins of my youth.*" It comforts me to think of that in relation to my teens. *They know not what they do.*

But most of all, my never-ending goal is to be like the mother in Loretta Lynn's song, "The Coal Miner's Daughter." This mother did not grumble, despite poverty, hard work, and constant cares. Loretta summed it up in one simple phrase, "*To complain there was no need. She'd smile in Mommy's understanding way.*"

I have been greatly encouraged by the writings of Mother Teresa. This quote, in particular, is the solution to feeling unappreciated:

"In the final analysis, it is between you and God. It was never between you and them anyway."

Childhood Home As The Nursery

Sometimes my grown children get homesick. They miss the days of the nursery - where Mother is here for them all the time. When Mother bakes cookies, makes supper and plays games. It is the soothing seclusion of a loving home - where the world is shut out for a time.

I can often see pain, in the eyes of my teenagers. But I cannot make it go away. I cannot stop them from hurting, or from suffering, in this life. But I can be here, with a loving smile and open arms.

I can listen to their stories. . . without judgment. . . I can hear their trials and tribulations and say nothing. This is the resting place. Home is the place to recover from the world. But I cannot make the world go away.

So I play cards with them. . We gather around the table and we laugh and have a good time. We all have hurt in our eyes, but we push it aside.

And we play pool, in our beat up, unfinished porch that we call the game room. We play on teams and I hear stories and jokes and I hear things I never thought could be so funny! I enjoy my teenagers and grown children. But I do not try to run their lives. I do not try to control them.
I am the keeper of the nursery.

Come here, my precious babies, when the world has become too painful. . . Come home to the nursery, where I will always be - with the cookies and the cards and the loving smile.

(Love, Mom.)

Mother As The Coach

Ray Charles went blind when he was 5 years old. His mother was a devout Christian. They lived in a poor community and she had to train him for life. Did she know she was going to die when he was 15? Probably not. But she knew she had to help him to live in a difficult world.

I remember watching his life story on television. I remember seeing this small, precious boy calling for his mother. He had recently gone blind. He needed help. I remember seeing that wise woman standing off in a corner watching him. She just watched. That boy called and called and it broke her heart. She wouldn't answer because she was teaching him. Thinking he was alone, he started to listen to the sounds around him. He started to reach out and see where he was walking. He started to actually *live* blind. His mother had tears on her cheeks. He was learning.

- - - - - - - - - - - - - - - - - - - -

A Coach is someone who trains the team. He trains the players to succeed and to win. A Mother is a coach in her own home. She teaches her children how to get along, how to form a family team, and how to survive out in the real world.

Sibling Rivalry

The coach wants the team to be a family. They need to have each other's backs. There has to be compassion and caring and kindness. No one is closer than a brother. No one will sacrifice more for a brother. A brother will work despite pain, for the benefit of a suffering team-mate. Yes, all children argue. Yes, they have their moments of feeling left out or that someone else is the favorite; but when trials come, when the games (in life) are being played, and the storms are brewing, the team pulls together and forms a bond which is not easily broken. As for my own children, they have given up hard earned cash to help each other. They have willingly worked to pay for a designer coat, or a snack, or a special birthday gift to cheer the other. When times are hard, each one will give anything to take care of the other. They are the team-mates in the White House who were coached by Mother.

Work Ethic

I required all my children to work hard. Each one had a job. I encouraged them to move fast and get the job done. When all the children were young, this was easier because they would compete with one another. They would see who could run faster, who could lift more grocery bags and who could have the cleanest room. (They did this on their own, to make the work fun.) But my youngest had it harder. I had to train him without the benefit of co-laborers. I would have him open doors for me (learn to be a gentleman), even while he was holding grocery bags. I would have him bring all the heavy shopping bags into the house - alone. He did not understand this, but my praises and my kindness made him realize I was teaching him how to work. All my children have a tremendous work ethic.

On the Field

I have taught my children morals and values. I have advised them through some difficult times. But they don't always listen to me. Children will not always listen to their coach. But, know this, when they get out on the field, and they try it their own way - the players and the crowds (the world) will teach them. Your student may come back harmed, limping and sore. But he will understand your lessons.

Resenting the Coach

Often the coach must be stern. The coach must carefully push the players to a point where their accomplishments exceed their own dreams. We Mothers don't want our children lazing around the house, being pampered by us. We don't want them to slack, or get away with living an unproductive life. So we provide training opportunities. We provide work and see that it is carried out. In the beginning, the team will grumble and gripe, but as they rise and succeed, they appreciate and love their coach. They see that it was not all in vain. Many have come back to say, "Coach, thank you for making me work. Thank you for putting up with me and standing beside me all these years and never giving up on me."

The retired years of a Mother Coach are the most precious of all. She sees the fruit of her labors. She sees those children coming back from the battlefield (life) with war stories and victories! She sees them as productive citizens who have learned life lessons. Her hair is white from age. Her vision is fading. But her team loves and respects her with great admiration.

Mama's Songs

My Father is from the *old South* in Alabama. His father was a revival preacher. Dad was a street-preacher as a teenager and his brother was a preacher as well. Later, my Uncle had his own church.

Dad moved to New England, where we children grew up. But we would make the trip to Alabama to visit the family and go to church. Those were the most precious sermons I've ever heard. So many people would have tears in their eyes. The old gospel songs were beautiful. They were old country songs, sung from the hymn book by God's dear humble children.

Back at home, Dad would sing these songs throughout the house all the time. He sang from his heart and I loved to hear him. I have never seen him sing on stage, but his music taught me so much. The lyrics about Mama's Prayers, and Walking the Golden Stairs to Heaven made a deep impression on me.

I remember once asking Dad if he would record his voice onto a cassette tape for me, so I could memorize the words. He did this, but when I listened to it, it made me cry. Soon, I was able to hear the songs and transcribe the lyrics. I learned these old songs the way Daddy sang them.

Now I sing in my own home, in my own humble way and my children hear me. John (12) will sit and sing with me. The children all hear me and it is getting into their hearts. No matter what happens in their lives, they will remember their childhood and Mama's voice, singing those old gospel songs.

One day, some time ago, Nicole (20) told me something she remembered from her childhood. She remembered my songs about going to Heaven and she thought that was the sweetest, most comforting memory.

Sitting Alone at The Kitchen Table

The other night, I carefully placed a white lace tablecloth on my kitchen table. I was making dinner and making things look lovely for the evening meal.. . But no one was around.

I listened to soothing music and put a pretty candle on the center of the table. Then I put plates, napkins and silverware in each place. . . I did this, knowing everyone was out or busy.

When the food was ready, I created a nice presentation on my dinner plate and walked over to a chair at the table. *I sat there all alone and ate.* It was a lovely meal.

My teenagers and husband came and went. They ate quickly or not at all. They were busy. They had jobs or events they needed to go to.

On holidays, I like to read to the children and have some time together. But they rush through the events, saying gently, "We are not kids anymore," or "We have other plans." They are busy, growing up and having their own lives. This *is normal.*

Instead of feeling sad when they don't have time to help bake cookies, or make a special meal, or sit while I read to them, I do it myself and smile. Yes, I read to myself. I bake on my own, and I sit at the beautifully- set table alone.

I do this because it is stable. It brings me joy. . . They all see I am doing this. They rush through their lives, but they can still see what I am doing. And they know *they are always welcome at the table*, whenever life slows down for them.

I will not change because they are busy. I will not stop setting the table or making special meals, because they *need to know* those things will always be waiting for them when they need it.

Because one day, when they have grown up, they will remember that mother always does these same things, whether they are able to join me or not. Whether they are busy or not, mother will be sitting at the kitchen table.

They will remember that, despite the hustle and bustle of life, *Mother* and *Home* are stable.

Last night, as I sat at my kitchen table, I thought of my religion. I thought of how *times* and *culture* change, but my faith must stay the same. I thought of how people get too busy to do the most basic foundational things that keep their spirits joyful and their hearts warm with love. And I realized that by sitting at the kitchen table, *even if I am alone,* it is similar to how I must keep my religious duties, even if no one else does.

What Sundays Used to Mean to Housewives

The Housewife of old used to look forward to Sunday Morning. She would spend the morning in delightful anticipation of fellowship and Church services. This dear mother would get all dressed up in her best and help the family get ready. As she walked out that door, with Bible in hand, she would take one last look around and know that her work at home had been done well. It was time to rest. It was time to be refreshed and take a break from the world and all its trials and labors.

I like to think of going to church each week as an example of the end of our lives. During the week, we housewives do all our work. We do laundry, wash floors, make meals, handle appointments, phone calls, shopping, bills, and heavy cleaning. *This is our labor in the world.* When that church day arrives, we take a much deserved rest. We have our reward.

To me, the end of my life will be like Mother's day. I will be sitting in a church pew with my dear husband beside me. All our grown children will have put aside their wanderings in the world and will be there with me. They will have the hearts of humble servants and everyone will be grateful to be there. The precious sermon will start. . . Yet there will be tears welling up in my eyes because all my children are with me. *They made it!* And it will be just like the way it was supposed to be all along.

~ ~ ~ ~

"For my part," said Apelles, "I envy those who love and feast upon the Bible; for, though I speak it with shame, I am lacking in that love. I read a passage every day, of course, in my closet, and again in my family, but not as my old father did. Once, when he thought himself unobserved, he has been seen to press the sacred book to his lips. And on her death-bed, my mother called for hers, and took leave of it as tenderly as she said farewell to her children."

– Elizabeth Prentiss (1800's) from her book, "Urbane and His Friends."

About the Author:

Mrs. White is the Mother of 5 children and a Grandmother of 2. She has been homeschooling for more than 20 years. She and her husband live in an old 1800's house in rural Vermont.

Her Blog, "The Legacy of Home," was created in April of 2009 and was designed to encourage homemakers and homeschoolers to have peaceful, godly homes.

Visit her at:
http://thelegacyofhome.blogspot.com

Made in the USA
Las Vegas, NV
21 January 2022